# Signing at School

## SIGN LANGUAGE FOR KIDS

by Kathryn Clay

illustrated by Margeaux Lucas

**Consultant:** Kari Sween
Adjunct Instructor of
American Sign Language
Minnesota State University, Mankato

CAPSTONE PRESS
a capstone imprint

# TABLE OF CONTENTS

# How to Use This Guide

This book is full of useful words in both English and American Sign Language (ASL). The English word and sign for each word appear next to the picture. Arrows are used to show movement for some signs.

Most ASL signs are understood wherever you go. But some signs may change depending on where you are. It's like having a different accent.

**For example, New Yorkers sign "pizza" like this:**

**People in other places might sign "pizza" like this:**

or this:

People will not understand you if they can't see your signs. Make sure your hands are always in view when signing with someone. Don't be afraid to ask people to slow down or sign again if you don't understand a sign.

# Brief Introduction to American Sign Language (ASL)

Many people who are deaf or hard of hearing use ASL to talk. Hearing people may also learn ASL to communicate with deaf friends and family members.

Signs can be very different from one another. Signs may use one or both hands. Sometimes signs have more than one step. For other signs, you must move your entire body. If there is no sign for a word, you can fingerspell it.

People use facial expressions when they sign. They smile when signing good news. They frown when signing sad news. Body language is also important. Someone might sign slowly to show that he or she is very tired.

It's important to remember that learning to sign is like learning any language. ASL becomes easier with practice and patience.

# Alphabet Chart

ASL has a sign for every letter of the English alphabet. If there is no sign for a word, you can use letter signs to spell out the word. Fingerspelling is often used to sign the names of people and places.

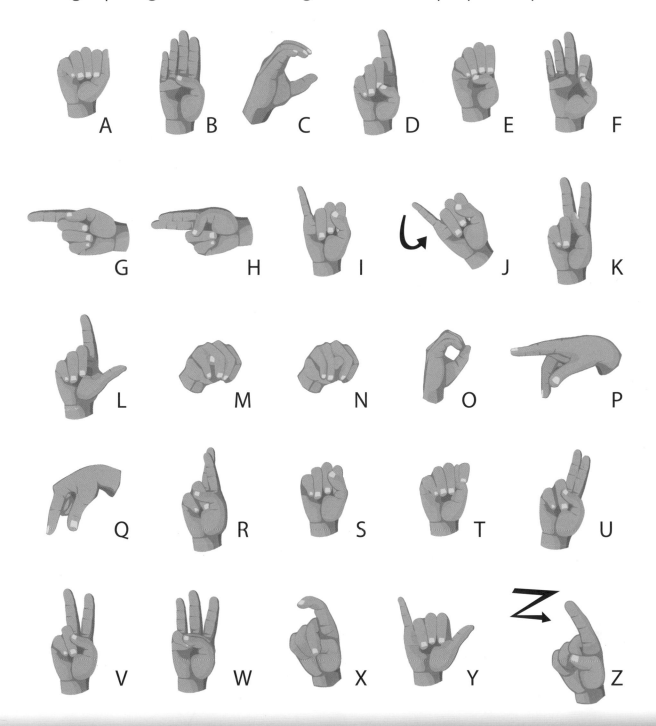

# BUS STOP

1. Fingerspell B-U-S.
2. Bring hand down to palm.

## backpack
Tap chest twice with thumbs.

## homework
1. Move hand up cheek.
2. Tap wrists together once.

## bench
Slide top fingers away from body.

## sit
Tap fingers once.

## sign
Draw a square with fingers.

## sidewalk
Move hands away from body.

# CLASSROOM

1. Make C shapes and move in a circle.
2. Make a box shape.

**desk** Tap arms together twice.

## pencil

Place finger near mouth. Slide fingers across palm.

**teacher**
1. Move hands away from forehead.
2. Open hands and move them down body.

## crayon
Wiggle fingers on chin. Pretend to draw.

## paper
Slide palms together twice.

## map
1. Fingerspell M-A-P
2. Pretend to open map and draw a circle.

9

# LIBRARY

Move L shape in a circle.

**book** Open hands like opening a book.

**read** Slide fingers across palm.

**librarian**
1. Move L shape in a circle.
2. Open hands and move them down body.

**quiet** Move hands away from mouth.

**computer** Slide C shape up arm.

**student**
1. Make flat O shape and move hand from palm to forehead.
2. Open hands and move them down body.

# CAFETERIA

Make C shape and touch both corners of chin.

**tray** Move wrists forward.

**apple** Wiggle X shape at corner of mouth.

**loud** 1. Point to ear. 2. Shake fists.

**sandwich** Bring hand in between thumb and pointer finger.

**milk** Squeeze fingers together.

**hungry** Make C shape and move hand down chest.

**thirsty** Point to chin and move finger down throat.

# PLAYGROUND

1. Make Y shapes and shake hands.
2. Move hand in a circle.

**basketball**    Move wrists forward twice.

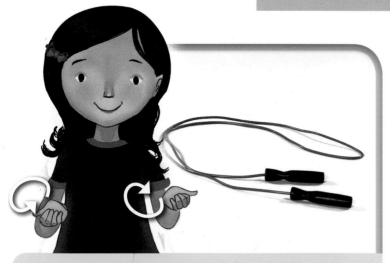

**jump rope**    Make A shapes and move wrists in a circle.

**game**    Make A shape and tap knuckles together twice.

**football** Lace fingers together twice.

**slide** Move top hand down and away from bottom hand.

**swing** Move hands forward.

**hopscotch** Tap fingers once then spread apart.

# SUBJECTS

Bend fingers.

**math**  Make M shapes and cross.

**science**  Make A shapes. Circle hands near chest but not touching.

**history**  Make H shape and shake fingers twice.

**music**   Move hand back and forth along arm.

**art**   Wiggle pinky down palm.

**English**   Grab bottom hand and move toward body.

# NUMBERS

Touch fingertips twice
while twisting wrists.

**0**

**1**

**2**

**3**

**4**

**5**

**6**

**7**

**8**

**9**

**10**

**100**

# COLORS

Wiggle fingers at chin.

**red** Touch lips and curl finger.

**yellow** Twist Y shape.

**blue** Twist B shape.

**green** Twist G shape.

**orange** Squeeze fingers together twice.

**purple** Twist P shape.

**black** Move finger across forehead.

**white** Move hand away from chest and bring fingers together.

**pink** Make P shape and slide down lips twice.

# SHAPES

Make A shapes and wiggle hands down body.

**circle** Draw a circle with finger.

**rectangle** Draw a rectangle with fingers.

**square** Draw a square with fingers.

**triangle** Draw a triangle with fingers.

**heart** Draw a heart on chest.

**star** Slide fingers back and forth.

# TELLING TIME

Tap wrist twice.

**morning** Move hand up and toward body.

**afternoon** Move hand away from body.

**night** Move hand down and away from body.

**week** Point finger and move hand across palm.

☐ Monday
☐ Tuesday
☐ Wednesday
☐ Thursday
☐ Friday
☐ Saturday
☐ Sunday

24

**month** Point finger and slide down hand.

**year** Make S shapes and move top hand in a circle.

**minute** Point finger and move wrist forward quickly.

**hour** Point finger and move hand in a circle.

# DAYS OF THE WEEK

Point finger and move hand across palm.

## Monday

Make M shape and move hand in a circle.

## Tuesday

Make T shape and move hand in a circle.

## Wednesday

Make W shape and move hand in a circle.

## Thursday

Make H shape and move hand in a circle.

## Friday

Make F shape and move hand in a circle.

## Saturday

Make S shape and move hand in a circle.

## Sunday

Move palms down.

# MONTHS

Point finger and slide down hand.

## January

Fingerspell J-A-N.

## February

Fingerspell F-E-B.

## March

Fingerspell M-A-R-C-H.

## April

Fingerspell A-P-R-I-L.

## May

Fingerspell M-A-Y.

## June

Fingerspell J-U-N-E.

## July
Fingerspell J-U-L-Y.

## August
Fingerspell A-U-G.

## September
Fingerspell S-E-P-T.

## October
Fingerspell O-C-T.

## November
Fingerspell N-O-V.

## December
Fingerspell D-E-C.

# GLOSSARY

**accent**—the way people say words differently based on where they live

**body language**—the act of sharing information by using gestures, movements, and facial expressions

**communicate**—to share thoughts, feelings, or information

**deaf**—unable to hear

**facial expression**—feelings shared by making different faces; making an angry face to show you are mad, for example

# BOOKS IN THIS SERIES

# READ MORE

**Nelson, Michiyo.** *Sign Language: My First 100 Words.*
New York: Scholastic, 2008.

**Petelinsek, Kathleen, and E. Russell Primm**.
*At School.* Talking Hands.
Chanhassen, Minn.: The Child's World, 2006.

**Schaefer, Lola M**. *Some Kids Are Deaf.*
Mankato, Minn.: Capstone Press, 2008.

# INTERNET SITES

FactHound offers a safe, fun way to find Internet sites related to this book. All of the sites on FactHound have been researched by our staff.

Here's all you do:

Visit *www.facthound.com*

Type in this code: 9781620650523

A+ Books are published by Capstone Press,
1710 Roe Crest Drive, North Mankato, Minnesota 56003
www.capstonepub.com

**Library of Congress Cataloging-in-Publication Data**
Clay, Kathryn.
 Signing at school : sign language for kids / by Kathryn Clay.
  pages cm.—(A+ books. Time to sign)
Summary: "Illustrations of American Sign Language, along with labeled
photos, introduce children to words and phrases useful for signing at
school"—Provided by publisher.
ISBN 978-1-62065-052-3 (library binding)
ISBN 978-1-4765-3357-5 (ebook PDF)
1. American Sign Language—Juvenile literature. 2. English language—
Alphabet—Juvenile literature. I. Title.
HV2480.C534 2014
372.6—dc23                        2013010639

**Editorial Credits**
Tracy Davies McCabe, designer; Svetlana Zhurkin, media researcher;
Kathy McColley, production specialist

**Photo Credits**
Capstone Studio: Karon Dubke, cover (bottom left), 7 (bottom left), 8, 9, 10, 11 (middle and bottom), 12, 13
(top left and bottom right), 14, 15, 16 (bottom left), 17, 24 (top left); iStockphotos: Bart van den Dikkenberg,
cover (middle left), Bastun, 3, 5; Shutterstock: AigarsR, 7 (top left), BortN66, 25 (bottom left), Daemys,
28 (bottom left), Daniel Padavona, 29 (top left), Daniel Sainthorant, 6 (bottom), David M. Schrader, 24
(bottom left), erdem, 25 (top right), fotohunter, 29 (top middle), Gemenacom, 25 (bottom right), Gianna
Stadelmyer, 28 (bottom right), graphit, 29 (bottom left and bottom right), Ilka Erika Szasz-Fabian, 16
(top), James R. Martin, 7 (bottom right), Kesu, 28 (bottom middle), Leyla Siyanova, 25 (top left),
Malchev, 28 (top right), Mary Voitikova, 28 (top middle), MaxyM, 29 (top right), Michelle D.
Milliman, 6 (top), Mike Flippo, 13 (top right), Monkey Business Images, 13 (bottom left), Natali
Glado, 29 (bottom middle), Nolte Lourens, 7 (top right), Petr Vaclavek, 28 (top left), Sealstep,
cover (top right), Thomas M. Perkins, 11 (top), Victorian Traditions, 16 (bottom right),
Voronin76, 24 (top right), zwola fasola, 24 (bottom right)

**Note to Parents, Teachers, and Librarians**
This accessible, visual guide uses full color photographs and illustrations
and inviting content to introduce young readers to American Sign Language.
The book provides an early introduction to reference materials and
encourages further learning by including the following sections:
Table of Contents, Alphabet Chart, Glossary, Read More, and
Internet Sites.

Printed in the United States of America in North Mankato, Minnesota.
032013      007223CGF13